First published by Koka Kids, 2020
Copyright © Nicola Fairbrother, 2020
Illustrations by Jose Obrador
www.kokakids.co.uk

All rights reserved. No part of this publication may be reproduced, stored in a retrieval system or transmitted in any form or by any means without prior written permission of Nicola Fairbrother.

Disclaimer: Judo is a fantastic sport for children to learn but there is a risk and judo techniques should only be attempted in the presence of a qualified judo coach in a dojo with appropriate facilities. Nicola Fairbrother or Koka Kids will not be held responsible for any injury, accident, loss or death resulting from reading or attempting techniques illustrated in this book. Every attempt has been made to ensure accuracy of this publication. No responsiblity can be accepted for errors or views expressed.

A MESSAGE FROM OLYMPIC SILVER MEDALLIST
NIK FAIRBROTHER

HAJIME!

We learn breakfalls so we can fall safely when we are thrown.

This book will teach you how to breakfall correctly in four ways; backwards, forwards, sideways and rolling.

Start by mastering these four breakfalls, then move on to the ten agility exercises I have set for you.

These exercises have been created to help you improve flexibility, coordination and balance.

Learn how to fall correctly and you will be able to attack with more confidence.

Good luck with your ukemi!

—BY—
NIK FAIRBROTHER MBE
WORLD CHAMPION 1993
OLYMPIC SILVER MEDALLIST 1992
TRIPLE EUROPEAN CHAMPION

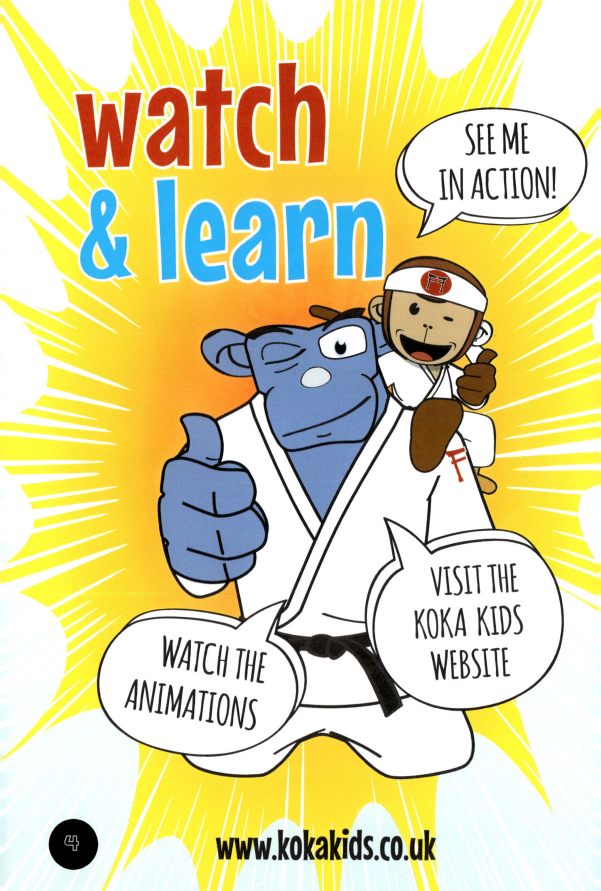

BEFORE WE BOW, BEFORE WE GRIP UP, BEFORE WE GO TO THE NEXT PAGE THERE ARE **THREE** IMPORTANT

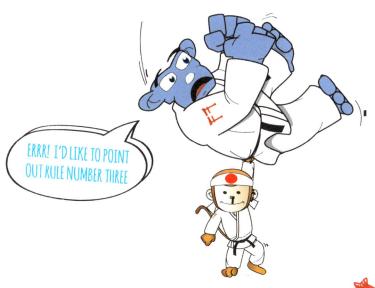

ERRR! I'D LIKE TO POINT OUT RULE NUMBER THREE

1 ASK YOUR COACH BEFORE TRYING ANY TECHNIQUE IN THIS BOOK.

2 ONLY DO JUDO IN A DOJO, WHEN YOUR COACH IS PRESENT.

3 TORI AND UKE ARE A TEAM AND SHOULD WORK TOGETHER.

 This book contains judo techniques and training exercises that should be done under supervision at all times. Your judo coach will be able to guide you to the techniques that suit your age and level. Please check with your judo coach before trying anything new.

BLUSHIDO

Blushido is as strong and powerful as he looks. But those muscles are packed with courage and kindness.

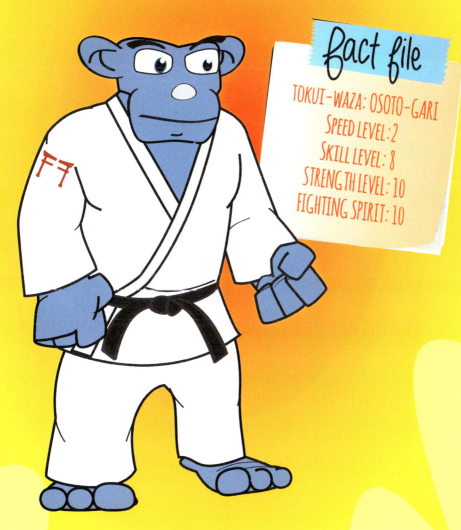

fact file
TOKUI-WAZA: OSOTO-GARI
SPEED LEVEL: 2
SKILL LEVEL: 8
STRENGTH LEVEL: 10
FIGHTING SPIRIT: 10

www.kokakids.co.uk

KATIE GATAME

Katie Gatame is a brown belt, and is the most technical of them all – she knows every waza in The Gokyo.

fact file

TOKUI-WAZA: KESA-GATAME
SPEED LEVEL: 7
SKILL LEVEL: 10
STRENGTH LEVEL: 8
FIGHTING SPIRIT: 10

www.kokakids.co.uk

ASHLEY GURUMA

Ashley Guruma is a natural ashi-waza expert.
Put your foot in the wrong place and he will sweep it away!

fact file

TOKUI-WAZA: ASHI-GURUMA
SPEED LEVEL: 9
SKILL LEVEL: 8
STRENGTH LEVEL: 8
FIGHTING SPIRIT: 9

www.kokakids.co.uk

Coach Zen's UKEMI TIPS

Always...

1. Tuck your chin in

2. Round your back

3. Hit the mat with an open palm

www.kokakids.co.uk

www.kokakids.co.uk

How to do Ushiro Ukemi

www.kokakids.co.uk

How to do Mae Ukemi

How to do Yoko Ukemi

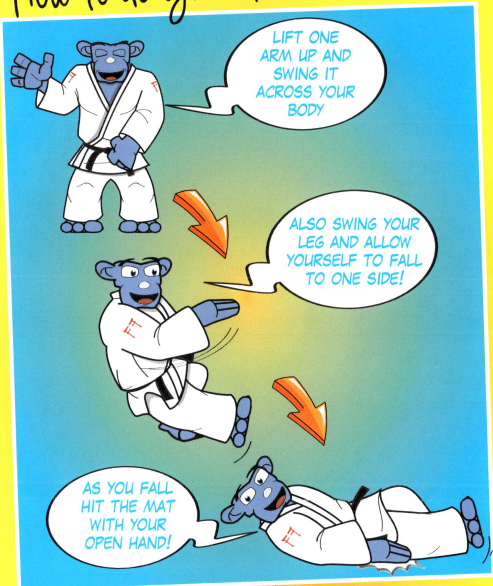

www.kokakids.co.uk

How to do Ukemi

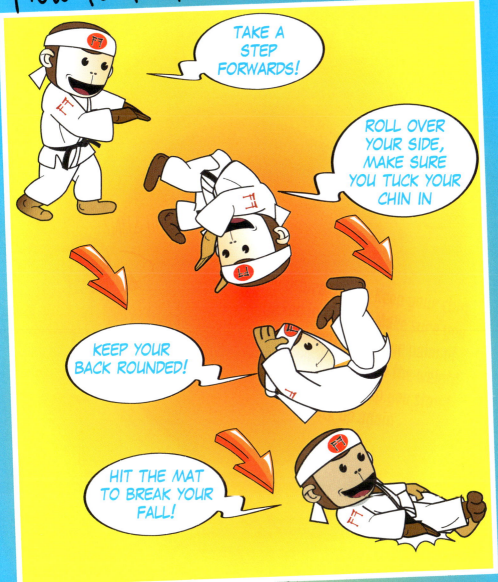

ROLL TO FEET

Can you keep the momentum going and roll back up to your feet? How many rolls can you do in 30 seconds?

Momentum

Do a forward breakfall (see page 21), but don't end the roll laying down on the tatami. Keep the roll going and return to your starting position. Repeat the length of the mat.

KEEP THE MOVEMENT GOING!

www.kokakids.co.uk

BACK TO FEET

Can you do a backwards breakfall and roll back to a standing position? Repeat 5 times without a mistake!

START & FINISH POSITION

Keep the rhythm

Do Ushiro Ukemi. Keep your chin tucked in tightly. Make sure you hit the mat with your palm of your hand. Then, use the weight of your legs to help you stand back up again.

USE YOUR LEGS TO HELP YOU!

www.kokakids.co.uk

TWIST OUT

Can you do a Mae Ukemi when uke attacks you with Osoto-Gari? Twist out and land on your forearms.

Be like a cat!

Cats always land on their front! You can too. Practise this move. Get your partner to attack you with Osoto-Gari. Let go and twist away from the throw to land on your front.

REACT QUICKLY!

TWIST AWAY FROM THE THROW

FINISH LIKE THIS!

www.kokakids.co.uk

DOJO DRILL — IN ACTION

What about if you are thrown? Are you still able to breakfall correctly in the midst of all the action?

Keep calm

Being thrown is a part of judo! A good uke should allow their partner to throw them. Get used to it and build confidence by practising your breakfalls from various heights and directions

TORI SHOULD HELP UKE LAND

HIT THE MAT WITH AN OPEN PALM

www.kokakids.co.uk

DOJO DRILL: DUO ROLL

This fun exercise takes courage to do. But work as a team and you'll soon be duo rolling down the mat!

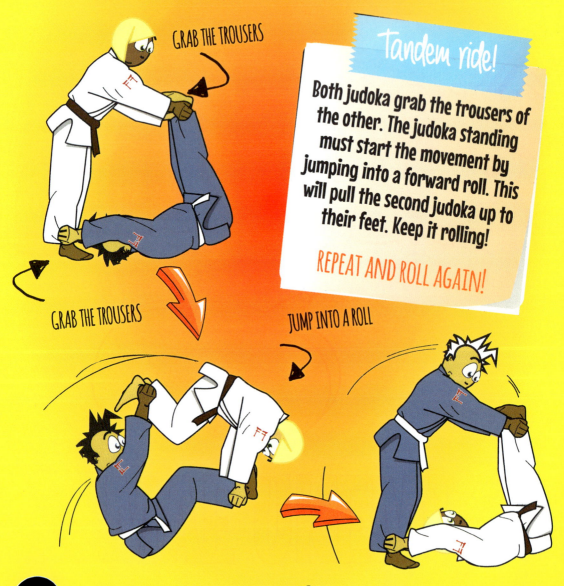

GRAB THE TROUSERS

GRAB THE TROUSERS

JUMP INTO A ROLL

Tandem ride!

Both judoka grab the trousers of the other. The judoka standing must start the movement by jumping into a forward roll. This will pull the second judoka up to their feet. Keep it rolling!

REPEAT AND ROLL AGAIN!

www.kokakids.co.uk

DOJO DRILL: HIGH DIVE

As you get more confident take your ukemi to new heights. Jump over objects or willing judoka!

Lift off!

Can you jump into a forward ukemi? Practise first onto a crash pad. Then place a small soft object on the mat and roll over that. Next ask your partner to curl up in a tight ball and roll over them!

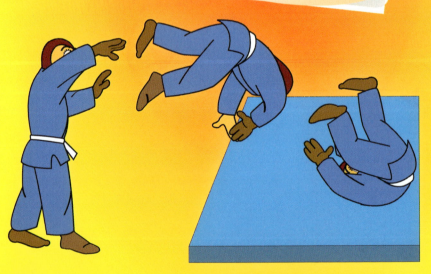

www.kokakids.co.uk

DOJO DRILL: SPRINT ROLLS

Sprinting builds up leg power and makes you fitter. How many shuttle rolls can you do in one minute?

On your marks!

Sprint from one side of the tatami to the other, touch the mat with your hand, turn and sprint back to the start. At some point during each sprint do a breakfall of your choice!

YOU BETTER LEG IT!

www.kokakids.co.uk

ROLL-KEMI

The next two agility tests are for advanced judoka so check with your coach first!

Get ready!

Uke does a forward roll. Tori should stand a good distance away. As uke stands up, tori moves in, takes a grip and turns in with Morote-Seoi-Nage.

IT'S ALL IN THE TIMING!

FORWARD UKEMI TO FEET

TAKE HOLD AND ATTACK

MOROTE SEOI-NAGE

www.kokakids.co.uk

DOJO DRILL: WAZA TEST

How many other forward throws can you think up and do from this exercise? Can get to ten techniques?

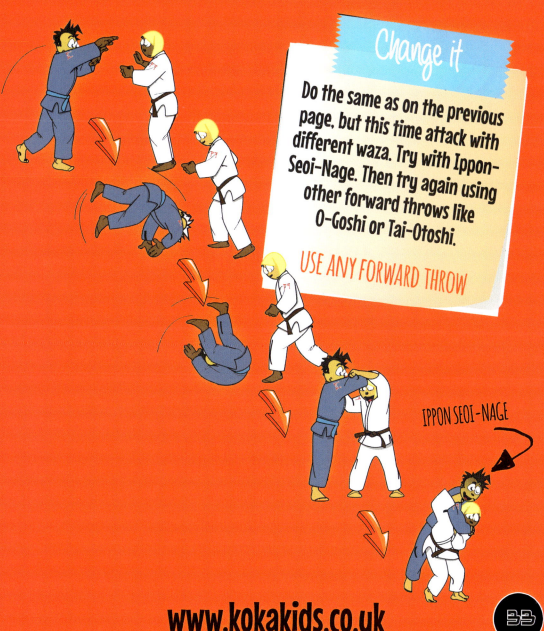

Change it

Do the same as on the previous page, but this time attack with different waza. Try with Ippon-Seoi-Nage. Then try again using other forward throws like O-Goshi or Tai-Otoshi.

USE ANY FORWARD THROW

IPPON SEOI-NAGE

www.kokakids.co.uk

If you have liked this book, please leave a review on Amazon, this helps promote judo and the books.

— BY —

NIK FAIRBROTHER MBE
WORLD CHAMPION 1993
OLYMPIC SILVER MEDALLIST 1992
TRIPLE EUROPEAN CHAMPION

MORE iN THE SERiES!

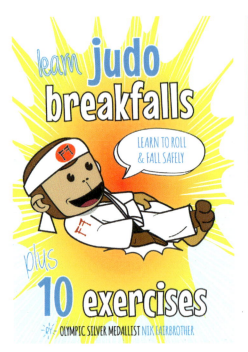
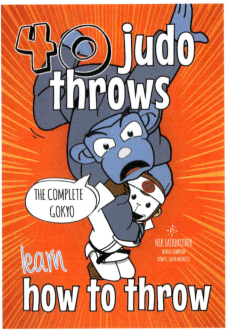
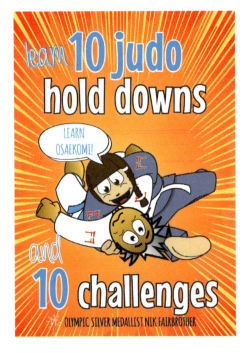
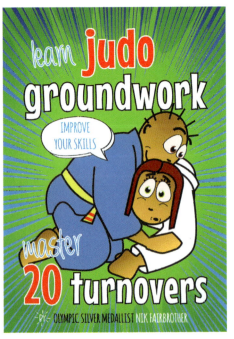

available at amazon

MORE IN THE SERIES!

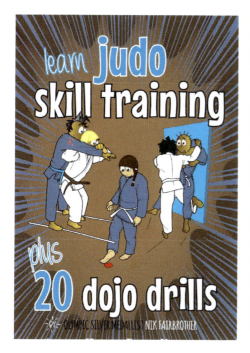
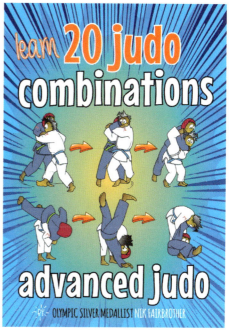
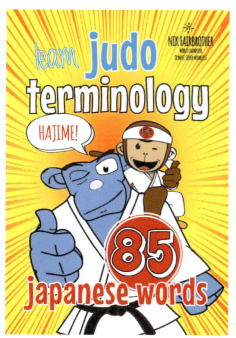
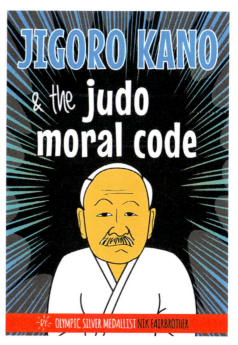

available at

JAPANESE WORDS

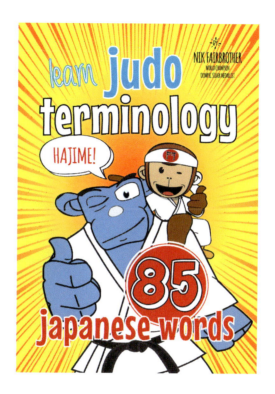

FREE E-BOOK

Don't know what a Japanese word means? That's OK - we have you covered!
Go to the Koka Kids website and download this free e-book. Learn 85 common Japanese judo words and their English meanings.

www.kokakids.co.uk

Printed in Great Britain
by Amazon